In the Year 1972

by

Kerry Butters.

In the Year 1972

Millennium: 2nd millennium

Centuries: 19th century – **20th century** – 21st century

Decades: 1940s 1950s 1960s – **1970s** – 1980s 1990s 2000s

Years: 1969 1970 1971 – **1972** – 1973 1974 1975

1972 (MCMLXXII) was a leap year starting on Saturday (dominical letter BA) of the Gregorian calendar, the 1972nd year of the Common Era (CE) and *Anno Domini* (AD) designations, the 972nd year of the 2nd millennium, the 72nd year of the 20th century, and the 3rd year of the 1970s decade.

Within the context of Coordinated Universal Time (UTC) it was the longest year ever, as two leap seconds were added during this 366-day year, an event which has not since been repeated. (If its start and end are defined using mean solar time [the legal time scale], its duration was 31622401.141 seconds of Terrestrial Time (or Ephemeris Time), which is slightly shorter than 1908).

Contents

Events

January

- January 1 – Kurt Waldheim becomes Secretary-General of the United Nations.
- January 2 – Pierre Hotel Robbery: Six men rob the safe deposit boxes of The Pierre hotel in New York City for at least $4 million.
- January 3 – MGM's 1951 *Show Boat* is presented on television by NBC for the first time. This marks the first complete network telecast of any version of *Show Boat* (it had already been filmed as a part-talkie in 1929, and as a full-sound musical in 1936).
- January 4
    - The first scientific hand-held calculator (HP-35) is introduced (price $395).
    - Rose Heilbron becomes the first woman judge at the Old Bailey in London.
- January 5 – U.S. President Richard Nixon orders the development of a Space Shuttle program.
-

- January 7
    - Iberia Airlines Flight 602 crashes into a 462-meter peak on the island of Ibiza; 104 are killed.
    - Howard Hughes speaks by telephone to denounce Clifford Irving's supposed biography of him.
- January 9 – The RMS *Queen Elizabeth* is destroyed by fire in Hong Kong harbor.
- January 10 – Sheikh Mujibur Rahman returns to Bangladesh from Pakistan.
- January 13 – Prime Minister of Ghana Kofi Abrefa Busia is overthrown in a military coup.
- January 14 – Queen Margrethe II of Denmark succeeds her father, King Frederick IX, on the throne of Denmark.
- January 19 – The Libertarian enclave Minerva on a platform in the South Pacific, sponsored by the Phoenix Foundation, declares independence. Soon neighboring Tonga annexes the area and dismantles the platform.
- January 20
    - President Zulfikar Ali Bhutto announces that Pakistan will immediately begin a nuclear weapons program.
    - Fears are growing about the economy of the United Kingdom, where unemployment is now exceeding 1 million for the first time since World War II.
- January 21
    - A New Delhi bootlegger sells wood alcohol to a wedding party; 100 die.
    - Tripura, part of the former independent Twipra Kingdom, becomes a full state of India.
- January 24 – Japanese soldier Shoichi Yokoi is discovered in Guam; he had spent 28 years in the jungle.

- January 25 – Shirley Chisholm, the first African American Congresswoman, announces her candidacy for President.
- January 26
  - Yugoslavian air stewardess Vesna Vulović is the only survivor when her plane crashes in Czechoslovakia. She survives after falling 10,160 meters (33,330 feet) in the tail section of the aircraft.
  - The Aboriginal Tent Embassy is set up on the lawn of Parliament House in Canberra.
- January 30
  - Bloody Sunday: The British Army kills 14 unarmed nationalist civil rights marchers in Derry, Northern Ireland.
  - Pakistan withdraws from the Commonwealth of Nations.
- January 31 – King Birendra succeeds his father as King of Nepal.

February

- February 2
  - A bomb explodes at the British Yacht Club in West Berlin, killing Irwin Beelitz, a German boat builder.
  - The German militant group 2 June Movement announces its support of the Provisional Irish Republican Army.
  - Anti-British riots take place throughout Ireland. The British Embassy in Dublin is burned to the ground, as are several British-owned businesses.
  - The last draft lottery is held, a watershed event in the wind-down of military conscription in the United

States during the Vietnam era. These draft candidates are never called to duty.

- February 3 – February 13 – The 1972 Winter Olympics are held in Sapporo, Japan.
- February 4 – *Mariner 9* sends pictures as it orbits Mars.
- February 5
  - U.S. airlines begin mandatory inspection of passengers and baggage.
  - Bob Douglas becomes the first African American elected to the Basketball Hall of Fame.
- February 9 – The British government declares a state of emergency over a miners' strike.
- February 15
  - President of Ecuador José María Velasco Ibarra is deposed for the fourth time.
  - Phonorecords are granted U.S. federal copyright protection for the first time.
- February 17 – Volkswagen Beetle sales exceed those of the Ford Model T when the 15,007,034th Beetle is produced.
- February 18 – The California Supreme Court voids the state's death penalty, commuting all death sentences to life in prison.
- February 19 – Asama-Sansō incident: Five United Red Army members break into a lodge below Mount Asama, taking the wife of the lodge keeper hostage.
- February 21 – The Soviet unmanned spaceship *Luna 20* lands on the Moon.
- February 21 – February 28 – U.S. President Richard M. Nixon makes an unprecedented 8-day visit to the People's Republic of China and meets with Mao Zedong.
-

- February 22
  - Aldershot Bombing: An Official IRA bomb kills 7 in Aldershot, England.
  - Lufthansa Flight 649 is hijacked and taken to Aden. Passengers are released the following day after a ransom of 5 million US dollars is agreed.
- February 23 – Angela Davis is released from jail. A Caruthers, California farmer, Rodger McAfee, helps her make bail.
- February 24 – North Vietnamese negotiators walk out of the Paris Peace Talks to protest U.S. air raids.
- February 26
  - A coal sludge spill kills 125 people in Buffalo Creek, West Virginia.
  - *Luna 20* comes back to Earth with 55 grams (1.94 oz) of lunar soil.
- February 28 – The Asama-Sanso incident ends in a standoff between 5 members of the Japanese United Red Army and the authorities, in which 2 policemen are killed and 12 injured.

March

- March 1
  - The Thai province Yasothon is created after being split off from the Ubon Ratchathani Province.
  - The Club of Rome publishes its report *The Limits to Growth*.
  - Juan María Bordaberry is sworn in as President of Uruguay amid accusations of election fraud.
  -

- March 2
  - The *Pioneer 10* spacecraft is launched from Cape Kennedy, to be the first man-made satellite to leave the solar system.
  - Jean-Bédel Bokassa becomes President of the Central African Republic.
- March 3 – Sculpted figures of Jefferson Davis, Robert E. Lee, and Stonewall Jackson are completed at Stone Mountain in the U.S. state of Georgia.
- March 4
  - Libya and the Soviet Union sign a cooperation treaty.
  - The Organisation of the Islamic Conference Charter is signed (effective 28 February 1973).
- March 5 – Greek composer Mikis Theodorakis leaves the Greek Communist Party.
- March 13
  - The United Kingdom and the People's Republic of China elevate diplomatic exchanges to the ambassadorial level after 22 years.
  - Clifford Irving admits to a New York court that he had fabricated Howard Hughes' "autobiography".
- March 16 – The first building of the Pruitt–Igoe housing development in St. Louis is destroyed.
- March 19 – India and Bangladesh sign the Indo-Bangladeshi Treaty of Friendship, Cooperation and Peace.
- March 22 – The 92nd U.S. Congress votes to send the proposed Equal Rights Amendment to the states for ratification.
- March 24
  - *The Godfather* is released in cinemas in the United States.

- The British government announces the prorogation of the Parliament of Northern Ireland and the introduction of 'Direct Rule' of Northern Ireland, after the Unionist government refuses to cede security powers.
- March 25 – "Après toi" sung by Vicky Leandros (music by Klaus Munro & Mario Panas, lyric by Klaus Munro & Yves Dessca) wins the Eurovision Song Contest 1972 for Luxembourg.
- March 26
  - An avalanche on Mount Fuji kills 19 climbers.
  - The last trolleybus system in the United Kingdom closes in Bradford, West Riding of Yorkshire after over 60 years of operation.
  - After 14 years, the last of Leonard Bernstein's *Young People's Concerts* is telecast by CBS. This last concert is devoted to Gustav Holst's *The Planets*.
- March 27 – The First Sudanese Civil War ends.
- March 30
  - Vietnam War: The Easter Offensive begins after North Vietnamese forces cross into the Demilitarized Zone (DMZ) of South Vietnam
  - The Parliament of Northern Ireland is suspended.

April

- April 7 – Vietnam War veteran Richard McCoy, Jr. hijacks a United Airlines jet and extorts $500,000; he is later captured.

- April 10
    - The U.S. and the Soviet Union join some 70 nations in signing the Biological Weapons Convention, an agreement to ban biological warfare.
    - Tombs containing bamboo slips, among them Sun Tzu's *Art of War* and Sun Bin's lost military treatise, are accidentally discovered by construction workers in Shandong.
    - A 7.0 Richter scale earthquake kills 5,000 people in the Iranian province of Fars.
    - The 44th Annual Academy Awards are held at the Dorothy Chandler Pavilion in Los Angeles.
- April 12 – The X-rated animated movie *Fritz the Cat* is released.
- April 13 – The Universal Postal Union decides to recognize the People's Republic of China as the only legitimate Chinese representative, effectively expelling the Republic of China administering Taiwan.
- April 16
    - *Apollo 16* (John Young, Ken Mattingly, Charlie Duke) is launched. During the mission, the astronauts achieve a lunar rover speed record of 18 km/h.
    - Vietnam War – Nguyen Hue Offensive: Prompted by the North Vietnamese offensive, the United States resumes bombing of Hanoi and Haiphong.
- April 17 – The first Boston Marathon in which women are officially allowed to compete.
- April 22 – Sylvia Cook and John Fairfax finish rowing across the Pacific.
- April 26 – The Lockheed L-1011 TriStar enters service with Eastern Airlines.

- April 27
  - The Burundian Genocide against the Hutu begins; more than 500,000 Hutus die.
  - A no-confidence vote against German Chancellor Willy Brandt fails under obscure circumstances.
- April 29 – The fourth anniversary of the Broadway musical *Hair* is celebrated with a free concert at a Central Park bandshell, followed by dinner at the Four Seasons. There, 13 Black Panther protesters and the show's co-author, Jim Rado, are arrested for disturbing the peace and for using marijuana.

May

- May 2 – Fire in a silver mine in Idaho kills 91.
- May 5 – An Alitalia DC-8 crashes west of Palermo, Sicily; 115 die.
- May 7 – General elections are held in Italy.
- May 8 – U.S. President Richard Nixon orders the mining of Haiphong Harbor in Vietnam.
- May 10 – Operation Linebacker and Operation Custom Tailor begin with large-scale bombing operations against North Vietnam by tactical fighter aircraft.
- May 13 – A Fire in a nightclub atop the Sennichi department store in Osaka, Japan, kills 115.
- May 15
  - Okinawa is returned to Japan after 27 years of United States occupation.
  - Governor George C. Wallace of Alabama is shot and paralyzed by Arthur Herman Bremer at a Laurel, Maryland, political rally.

- May 16 – The first financial derivatives exchange, the International Monetary Market (IMM), opens on the Chicago Mercantile Exchange.
- May 18 – Four troopers of the British Special Air Service and Special Boat Service are parachuted onto the ocean liner *Queen Elizabeth 2* 1,000 miles (1,600 km) across the Atlantic after a bomb threat and ransom demand which turn out to be bogus.
- May 19 – Three out of 6 bombs explode in the Axel Springer AG media company offices in Hamburg, Germany, injuring 17; the Red Army Faction claims responsibility.
- May 21 – In St. Peter's Basilica (Vatican City), Laszlo Toth attacks Michelangelo's *Pietà* statue with a geologist's hammer, shouting that he is Jesus Christ.
- May 22
  - The Dominion of Ceylon becomes the republic of Sri Lanka under prime minister Sirimavo Bandaranaike, when its new constitution is ratified.
  - Ferit Melen forms the new (interim) government of Turkey (35th government)
- May 23 – The Tamil United Front (later known as Tamil United Liberation Front), a pro-Tamil organization, is founded in Sri Lanka.
- May 24
  - Scottish Association football club Rangers F.C. win the UEFA Cup Winners' Cup, defeating FC Dynamo Moscow 3-2 in the final at Camp Nou in Barcelona (Spain). A pitch invasion by their supporters leads to the team being banned from defending the trophy the following season.

- A Red Army Faction bomb explodes in the Campbell Barracks of the U.S. Army Supreme European Command in Heidelberg, West Germany; 3 U.S. soldiers (Clyde Bonner, Ronald Woodard and Charles Peck) are killed.
  - The Magnavox Odyssey video game system is first demoed, marking the dawn of the video game age; it goes on sale to the public in August.
- May 26
  - Richard Nixon and Leonid Brezhnev sign the SALT I treaty in Moscow, as well as the Anti-Ballistic Missile Treaty and other agreements.
  - Wernher von Braun retires from NASA, frustrated by the agency's unwillingness to pursue a manned trans-orbital space program.
  - Willandra National Park is established in Australia.
- May 27 – Mark Donohue wins the Indianapolis 500 in the Penske Racing McLaren–Offenhauser.
- May 30
  - The Angry Brigade goes on trial in the United Kingdom.
  - Three Japanese Red Army members kill 24 and injure 100 in Lod Airport, Israel.

June

- June – Iraq nationalizes the Iraq Petroleum Company.
- June 2 – Andreas Baader, Jan-Carl Raspe, Holger Meins and some other members of the Red Army Faction are arrested in Frankfurt am Main after a shootout.
- June 3 – Sally Priesand becomes the first female U.S. rabbi.

- June 4 – Angela Davis is found not guilty of murder.
- June 5 – June 16 – The United Nations Conference on the Human Environment is held in Stockholm, Sweden
- June 8
    - Seven men and three women hijack a plane from Czechoslovakia to West Germany.
    - Vietnam War: Associated Press photographer Nick Ut takes his Pulitzer Prize-winning photograph of a naked nine-year-old Phan Thi Kim Phuc running down a road after being burned by napalm.
- June 9 – The Black Hills flood kills 238 in South Dakota.
- June 11 – Henri Pescarolo (France) and co-driver former World Drivers' Champion Graham Hill (Britain) win the 24 Hours of Le Mans in the Equipe Matra MS670.
- June 14 – June 23 – Hurricane Agnes kills 117 on the U.S. East Coast.
- June 14 – Japan Airlines Flight 471 crashes outside of New Delhi airport, killing 82 of 87 occupants.
- June 15 – Ulrike Meinhof and Gerhard Müller of the Red Army Faction are arrested in a teacher's apartment in Langenhagen, West Germany.
- June 15 – June 18 – The first U.S. Libertarian Party National Convention is held in Denver, Colorado.
- June 16 – 108 die as 2 passenger trains hit the debris of a collapsed railway tunnel near Soissons, France.
- June 17
    - Watergate scandal: Five White House operatives are arrested for burglarizing the offices of the Democratic National Committee.

- o The United States returns Okinawa, occupied and governed since the World War II Battle of Okinawa, to Japan.
- o Chilean president Salvador Allende forms a new government.
- June 18
  - o Staines air disaster: 118 die when a Trident 1 jet airliner crashes 2 minutes after take off from London Heathrow Airport.
  - o West Germany beats the Soviet Union 3–0 to win Euro 72.
  - o Hong Kong's worst flooding and landslides in recorded history with 653.2 millimetres (25.72 in) of rainfall in the previous 3 days. 67 people die due to building collapses in Mid-levels districts landslide and building collapses, with a further 83 due to flooding-related fatalities. It is the second worst fatality due to building collapses, and the worst flooding in Hong Kong's recorded history.
- June 23 – Watergate scandal: U.S. President Richard M. Nixon and White House chief of staff H. R. Haldeman are taped talking about using the C.I.A. to obstruct the F.B.I.'s investigation into the Watergate break-ins.
- June 26 – Nolan Bushnell and Ted Dabney co-found Atari.
- June 28 – U.S. President Richard Nixon announces that no new draftees will be sent to Vietnam.
- June 29 – *Furman v. Georgia*: The Supreme Court of the United States rules that capital punishment is unconstitutional.

- June 30 – The International Time Bureau adds the first leap second (23:59:60) to Coordinated Universal Time (UTC) at the end of the month.

July

- July – U.S. actress Jane Fonda tours North Vietnam, during which she is photographed sitting on a North Vietnamese anti-aircraft gun.
- July 1
  - The Canadian ketch *Vega*, flying the Greenpeace III banner, collides with the French naval minesweeper *La Paimpolaise* while in international waters, to protest French nuclear weapon tests in the South Pacific.
  - The Bureau of Alcohol, Tobacco and Firearms becomes independent from the IRS.
- July 2 – Following Pakistan's surrender to India in the Indo-Pakistani War of 1971, both nations sign the historic Simla Agreement, agreeing to settle their disputes bilaterally.
- July 4 – The first Rainbow Gathering is held in Colorado.
- July 8 – The U.S. sells grain to the Soviet Union for $750 million.
- July 10 – India's news agency reports that at least 24 people have been killed in separate incidents, in the Chandka Forest in India, by elephants crazed by heat and drought.
- July 10 – July 14 – The Democratic National Convention meets in Miami Beach. Senator George McGovern, who backs the immediate and complete withdrawal of U.S. troops from South Vietnam, is nominated for President. He names fellow Senator Thomas Eagleton as his running mate.

- July 15 – The Pruitt–Igoe housing development is demolished in St. Louis, Missouri.
- July 18 – Anwar Sadat expels 20,000 Soviet advisors from Egypt.
- July 21
  - Bloody Friday: 22 bombs planted by the Provisional IRA explode in Belfast, Northern Ireland; nine people are killed and 130 seriously injured.
  - Comedian George Carlin is arrested by Milwaukee police for public obscenity, for reciting his "Seven Words You Can Never Say On Television" at Summerfest.
  - A collision between two trains near Seville, Spain kills 76 people.
- July 23 – The United States launches Landsat 1, the first Earth-resources satellite.
- July 24 – King Jigme Singye Wangchuck succeeds his father Jigme Dorji Wangchuck as king of Bhutan.
- July 25 – U.S. health officials admit that African-Americans were used as guinea pigs in the Tuskegee Study of Untreated Syphilis in the Negro Male.
- July 27 – The McDonnell Douglas F-15 Eagle makes its first flight.
- July 28 – A national dock strike begins in Britain.
- July 31 – The Troubles, Northern Ireland:
  - Operation Motorman 4:00 AM: The British Army begins to regain control of the "no-go areas" established by Irish republican paramilitaries in Belfast, Derry ("Free Derry") and Newry.
  - Claudy bombing ("Bloody Monday"), 10:00 AM: Three car bombs in Claudy, County Londonderry, kill 9. It

becomes public knowledge only in 2010 that a local Catholic priest was an IRA officer believed to be involved in the bombings but his role was covered up by the authorities.

August

August 1 – U.S. Senator Thomas Eagleton, the Democratic vice-presidential nominee, withdraws from the race after revealing he was once treated for mental illness.

- August 4
  - Arthur Bremer is jailed for 63 years for shooting George Wallace.
  - Dictator Idi Amin declares that Uganda will expel 50,000 Asians with British passports to Britain within 3 months.
  - A huge solar flare (one of the largest ever recorded) knocks out cable lines in U.S. It begins with the appearance of sunspots on August 2; an August 4 flare kicks off high levels of activity until August 10.
- August 10 – A brilliant, daytime meteor skips off the Earth's atmosphere due to an Apollo asteroid streaking over the western US into Canada.
- August 14 – An East German Ilyushin airliner crashes near East Berlin; all 156 on board perish.
- August 16 – As part of a coup attempt, members of the Royal Moroccan Air Force fire upon, but fail to bring down, Hassan II of Morocco's plane while he is traveling back to Rabat.

- August 21 – The Republican National Convention in Miami Beach, Florida renominates U.S. President Richard Nixon and Vice President Spiro Agnew for a second term.
- August 22
  - Rhodesia is expelled by the IOC for its racist policies.
  - John Wojtowicz, 27, and Sal Naturile, 18, hold several Chase Manhattan Bank employees hostage for 17 hours in Gravesend, Brooklyn, N.Y. (an event later dramatized in the film *Dog Day Afternoon*).
  - In the Almirante Zar Naval Base, Argentina, 16 detainees are executed by firing squad in the Trelew massacre.
- August 26 – September 11 – The 1972 Summer Olympics are held in Munich, West Germany.

September

- September 1
  - Bobby Fischer defeats Boris Spassky in a chess match in Reykjavík, Iceland, becoming the first American world chess champion.
  - The Second Cod War begins between the United Kingdom and Iceland.
- September 4 – The first episode of *The Price Is Right* is aired on CBS by Bob Barker. *Gambit* and *The Joker's Wild* also premiere.
- September 5 – September 6 – Munich massacre: Eleven Israeli athletes at the 1972 Summer Olympics in Munich are murdered after 8 members of the Arab terrorist group Black September invade the Olympic Village; 5 guerillas and 1 policeman are also killed in a failed hostage rescue.

- September 10 – The Brazilian driver Emerson Fittipaldi wins the Italian Grand Prix at Monza and becomes the youngest Formula One World Champion.
- September 14 – West Germany and Poland renew diplomatic relations.
- September 17
    - Uganda announces that there are Tanzanian troops in its territory.
    - The television series *M*A*S*H* begins its run on CBS.
- September 18 – São Paulo Metro is inaugurated in Brazil.
- September 19 – A parcel bomb sent to the Israeli Embassy in London kills 1 diplomat.
- September 21 – Philippine president Ferdinand Marcos issues Proclamation No. 1081 placing the entire country under martial law.
- September 24 – An F-86 fighter aircraft leaving an air show at Sacramento Executive Airport fails to become airborne and crashes into a Farrell's Ice Cream Parlour, killing 12 children and 11 adults.
- September 25 – Norwegian EC referendum, 1972: Norway rejects membership in the European Economic Community.
- September 28 – The Canadian national men's hockey team defeats the Soviet national ice hockey team in Game 8 of the 1972 Summit Series (French: La Série du Siècle, Russian: Суперсерия СССР — Канада), 6–5, to win the series 4–3–1.
- September 29 – Sino-Japanese relations: The Joint Communiqué of the Government of Japan and the Government of the People's Republic of China is signed in Beijing, which normalizes diplomatic relations with the People's Republic of China after breaking official ties with the Republic of China (Taiwan).

- October – The government of former President of Somalia Mohamed Siad Barre formally introduces the Somali alphabet as Somalia's official writing script.
- October 1
  - The first publication reporting the production of a recombinant DNA molecule marks the birth of modern molecular biology methodology.
  - Alex Comfort's bestselling manual *The Joy of Sex* is published.
- October 2 – Denmark joins the European Community; the Faroe Islands stay out.
- October 5 – The United Reformed Church is founded out of the Congregational and Presbyterian Churches.
- October 6 – A train crash in Saltillo, Mexico kills 208 people.
- October 8
  - A major breakthrough occurs in the Paris peace talks between Henry Kissinger and Lê Đức Thọ.
  - R. Sargent Shriver is chosen to replace Thomas Eagleton as the U.S. vice-presidential nominee of the Democratic Party.
- October 12 – En route to the Gulf of Tonkin, an anti-war protest, the USS Kitty Hawk riot led by African-Americans and interpreted by some as a race riot involving more than 200 sailors, breaks out aboard the United States Navy aircraft carrier USS *Kitty Hawk*; nearly 50 sailors are injured.
- October 13 – Uruguayan Air Force Flight 571: A Fairchild FH-227D passenger aircraft transporting a rugby union team crashes at about 14,000' in the Andes mountain range, near

the Argentina/Chile border. Sixteen of the survivors are found alive December 20 but they have had to resort to cannibalism to survive.

- October 16
    - A plane carrying U.S. Congressman Hale Boggs of Louisiana and 3 other men vanishes in Alaska. The wreckage has never been found, despite a massive search at the time.
    - Rioting Maze Prison inmates cause a fire that destroys most of the camp.
- October 17 – Elizabeth II visits Yugoslavia.
- October 25
    - The first female FBI agents are hired.
    - Belgian Eddy Merckx sets a new world hour record in cycling in Mexico City.
- October 26 – Following a visit to South Vietnam, U.S. National Security Advisor Henry Kissinger suggests that "peace is at hand."
- October 28 – The Airbus A300 flies for the first time.
- October 29 – Lufthansa Flight 615 is hijacked and threats are made to be blown up if the three surviving perpetrators of the Munich massacre are not released from prison in West Germany. The demands are accepted, leading to fierce condemnation by Israel.
- October 30
    - U.S. President Richard Nixon approves legislation to increase Social Security spending by US$5.3 billion.
    - A commuter train collision in Chicago kills 45, injures hundreds.

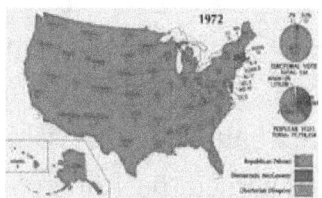

Nixon's landslide victory in the electoral college during the 1972 Election.

The arcade version of *Pong* is released.

- November
  - At a scientific meeting in Honolulu, Herbert Boyer and Stanley N. Cohen conceive the concept of recombinant DNA. They publish their results in November 1973 in PNAS. Separately in 1972, Paul Berg also recombines DNA in a test tube. Recombinant DNA technology has

dramatically changed the field of biological sciences, especially biotechnology, and opened the door to genetically modified organisms.

  ○ The Nishitetsu Lions baseball club, part of the NPB's Pacific League, is sold to the Fukuoka Baseball Corporation, a subsidiary of Nishi-Nippon Railroad. The team is renamed the Taiheiyo Club Lions.

- November 5 – A group of Amerindians occupies the Bureau of Indian Affairs.
- November 7 – U.S. presidential election, 1972: Republican incumbent Richard Nixon defeats Democratic Senator George McGovern in a landslide (the election had the lowest voter turnout since 1948, with only 55 percent of the electorate voting).
- November 8 – the oldest and longest continuously operating pay television service in the United States, HBO, is launched.
- November 11 – Vietnam War – Vietnamization: The United States Army turns over the massive Long Binh military base to South Vietnam.
- November 14 – The Dow Jones Industrial Average closes above 1,000 (1,003.16) for the first time.
- November 16 – The United Nations Educational, Scientific and Cultural Organization adopts the Convention Concerning the Protection of the World Cultural and Natural Heritage
- November 19 – Seán Mac Stíofáin, a leader of the Provisional Irish Republican Army, is arrested in Dublin after giving an interview to RTÉ.
- November 22 – Vietnam War: The United States loses its first B-52 Stratofortress of the war.

- November 28 – The last executions in Paris, France. Roger Bontems and Claude Buffet – the Clairvaux Mutineers – are guillotined at La Santé Prison by chief executioner André Obrecht (already suffering from Parkinson's disease). Bontems had been found innocent of murder by the court, but as Buffet's accomplice is condemned to death anyway. President Georges Pompidou, in private an abolitionist, upholds both death sentences in deference to French public opinion.
- November 29
  - Atari kicks off the first generation of video games with the release of their seminal arcade version of *Pong*, the first game to achieve commercial success.
  - The "tea house" Mellow Yellow opens on the Amstel River in Amsterdam, pioneering the legal sale of cannabis in the Netherlands.
- November 30
  - Vietnam War: White House Press Secretary Ron Ziegler tells the press that there will be no more public announcements concerning United States troop withdrawals from Vietnam, due to the fact that troop levels are now down to 27,000.
  - Cod War: British Foreign Secretary Sir Alec Douglas-Home says that Royal Navy ships will be stationed to protect British trawlers off Iceland.

December

- December 2 – Edward Gough Whitlam becomes the first Labor Party Prime Minister of Australia for 23 years. He is sworn in on 5 December and his first action using executive power is to withdraw all Australian personnel from the Vietnam War.

- December 7
  - *Apollo 17* (Gene Cernan, Ronald Evans, Harrison Schmitt), the last manned Moon mission to date, is launched and "The Blue Marble" photograph of the Earth is taken.
  - The Provisional Irish Republican Army kidnaps Jean McConville in Belfast.
  - Imelda Marcos is stabbed and seriously wounded by an assailant; her bodyguards shoot him.
- December 8
  - United Airlines Flight 553 crashes short of the runway, killing 43 of 61 passengers and 2 people on the ground.
  - Over $10,000 cash is found in the purse of Watergate conspirator Howard Hunt's wife.
  - International Human Rights Day is proclaimed by the United Nations.
- December 11– Apollo 17 lands on the Moon.
- December 14 – Apollo program: Eugene Cernan is the last person to walk on the moon, after he and Harrison Schmitt complete the third and final Extra-vehicular activity (EVA) of Apollo 17. This is the last manned mission to the moon of the 20th century.
- December 15
  - The Commonwealth of Australia ordains equal pay for women.
  - The United Nations Environment Programme is established as a specialized agency of the United Nations.
  -

- December 16
    - The Constitution of Bangladesh comes into effect.
    - The Portuguese army kills 400 Africans in Tete, Mozambique.
- December 19 – Apollo program: *Apollo 17* returns to Earth, concluding the program of lunar exploration.
- December 21
    - East Germany and West Germany recognize each other.
    - ZANLA troopers attack Altera Farm in north-east Rhodesia.
- December 22
    - Australia establishes diplomatic relations with China and East Germany.
    - A peace delegation that includes singer-activist Joan Baez and human rights attorney Telford Taylor visit Hanoi to deliver Christmas mail to American prisoners of war (they will be caught in the Christmas bombing of North Vietnam).
- December 23
    - A 6.25 Richter scale earthquake in Nicaragua kills 5,000–12,000 people in the capital, Managua; President Anastasio Somoza Debayle is later accused of pocketing millions of dollars worth of foreign aid intended for relief.
    - The Pittsburgh Steelers win their first ever post-season NFL game, defeating the Oakland Raiders 13–7, on a last second play that becomes known as The Immaculate Reception.
    - Swedish Prime minister Olof Palme compares the American bombings of North Vietnam to Nazi

massacres. The U.S. breaks diplomatic contact with Sweden.

- December 25 – The Christmas bombing of North Vietnam causes widespread criticism of the U.S. and President Richard Nixon.
- December 26 – Former United States President Harry S. Truman dies in Kansas City, Missouri.
- December 28 – The bones of Martin Bormann are identified in Berlin.
- December 29 – Eastern Air Lines Flight 401 crashes into the Everglades in Florida, killing 101 of 176 on board.
- December 31
  - Roberto Clemente dies in a plane crash off the coast of Puerto Rico while en route to deliver aid to Nicaraguan earthquake victims.
  - An extra leap second (23:59:60) is added to end the year.
  - The US ban on the pesticide DDT takes effect.

Date unknown

- The *International Year of the Book* is designated by UNESCO.
- The last major epidemic of smallpox in Europe breaks out in Yugoslavia.
- The United Kingdom begin to train Special Air Service for anti-terrorist duties.
- The first women are admitted to Dartmouth College in the United States.
- Colombian looters find Ciudad Perdida but keep it a secret until the government reveals it in 1975.
- The Yellow River dries up for the first time in known history.

- Worship of Norse gods is officially approved in Iceland.
- The Climatic Research Unit is founded by climatologist Hubert Lamb at the University of East Anglia.
- The Socialist Federal Republic of Yugoslavia bans the cultural organization Matica hrvatska, founded in 1842.
- The German company SAP AG is founded.
- Kadir Nurman introduces a sandwich made with döner kebab meat as a fast-food item in Berlin.

Births

January

Jang Seo-hee

Amanda Peet

Sakis Rouvas

Lilian Thuram

- January 1
    - Yoon Chan, South Korean actor
    - Barron Miles, Canadian defensive back for the BC Lions in the CFL
    - Lilian Thuram, French football player
- January 4 – Brad Zavisha, Canadian ice hockey player
- January 5
    - Jang Seo-hee, South Korean actress
    - Sakis Rouvas, Greek recording, film and television artist; model; businessman and former pole vaulter
- January 10 – Thomas Alsgaard, Norwegian cross-country skier
- January 11 – Amanda Peet, American actress
- January 12 – Espen Knutsen, Norwegian hockey player
- January 13
    - Nicole Eggert, American actress
    - Yukiko Iwai, Japanese voice actress

- o Vitaly Scherbo, Belarusian gymnast
- January 15
  - o Il Mi Chung, South Korean golfer
  - o Claudia Winkleman, British television presenter
  - o Yang Yong-eun, South Korean golfer
- January 16
  - o Ruben Bagger, Danish footballer
  - o Ang Christou, Australian rules footballer
  - o Dameon Clarke, Canadian actor and voice actor
  - o Yuri Alekseevich Drozdov, Russian footballer
  - o Ezra Hendrickson, Vincentian footballer
  - o Salah Hissou, Moroccan long-distance runner
  - o Joe Horn, American football player
  - o Greg Page, Australian musician and actor
  - o Alen Peternac, Croatian footballer
- January 17 – Ken Hirai, Japanese singer and songwriter
- January 18 – Mike Lieberthal, American baseball player
- January 19 – Angham, Egyptian singer, record producer and actress
- January 21 – Billel Dziri, Algerian footballer
- January 22 – Romi Park, Japanese voice actress
- January 23
  - o Ewen Bremner, Scottish actor
  - o Marcel Wouda, Dutch swimmer
- January 27
  - o Wynne Evans, Welsh operatic tenor
  - o Mark Owen, British pop singer (Take That)
  - o Keith Wood, Irish rugby player
- January 29 – Matt Brandstein, American writer

February

Dana International

Jaromír Jágr

Billie Joe Armstrong

Valeria Mazza

Keith Ferguson

- February 2
  - Dana International, Israeli transsexual singer, Eurovision Song Contest 1998 winner
  - Klára Dobrev, wife of Hungarian Prime Minister Ferenc Gyurcsány
  - Hendrick Ramaala, South African long-distance runner
  - Hisashi Tonomura, Japanese musician
- February 3 – Jesper Kyd, Danish video game composer
- February 4 – Giovanni Silva de Oliveira, Brazilian footballer
- February 5
  - Mary, Crown Princess of Denmark
  - Koriki Chōshū, Japanese comedian
- February 8 – Big Show, American professional wrestler
- February 9
  - Crispin Freeman, American voice actor
  - Norbert Rózsa, Hungarian swimmer
- February 11
  - Craig Jones, American musician
  - Steve McManaman, British footballer
  - Kelly Slater, American professional surfer
- February 14
  - Drew Bledsoe, American football player

- o Rob Thomas, American singer-songwriter (Matchbox Twenty)
- February 15 – Jaromír Jágr, Czech hockey player
- February 16 – Jerome Bettis, American football player
- February 17
  - o Billie Joe Armstrong, American rock musician and lead singer/guitarist (Green Day)
  - o Philippe Candeloro, French figure skater
  - o Yuki Isoya, Japanese singer
  - o Valeria Mazza, Argentinean model and businesswoman
- February 19 – Malky Mackay, Scottish footballer
- February 21 – Seo Taiji, Korean musician
- February 22
  - o Michael Chang, American tennis player
  - o Claudia Pechstein, German speed-skater
- February 24
  - o Pooja Bhatt, Indian actress
  - o Richard Chelimo, Kenyan athlete (d. 2001)
- February 25 – Jaak Mae, Estonian cross-country skier
- February 26 – Keith Ferguson, American voice actor
- February 29
  - o Antonio Sabàto, Jr., Italian actor
  - o Dave Williams, American musician and singer of Drowning Pool (d. 2002)
  - o Saul Williams, American singer, poet and actor

March

Shaquille O'Neal

Mark Hoppus

Dane Cook

- March 3 – Darren Anderton, English footballer
- March 4
  - Pae Gil-su, North Korean gymnast
  - Ivy Queen, Puerto Rican-American actress, singer-songwriter and record producer
  - Jos Verstappen, Dutch race car driver
  -

- March 6
  - Shaquille O'Neal, African-American basketball player
  - Jaret Reddick, American singer-songwriter and guitarist
- March 9
  - Ronald Cheng, Hong Kong singer and actor
  - Spencer Howson, Australian radio announcer
  - Travis Lane Stork, American emergency room physician and television personality
- March 10
  - Takashi Fujii (Matthew Minami), Japanese television performer
  - Matt Kenseth, American race car driver
  - Michael Lucas, Russian gay pornographic actor and director
  - Timbaland, American record producer, songwriter and rapper
- March 15 – Mark Hoppus, American musician
- March 17
  - Mia Hamm, American soccer player
  - Paige Hemmis, American television personality
- March 18 – Dane Cook, American comedian
- March 21
  - Chris Candido, American professional wrestler (d. 2005)
  - Derartu Tulu, Ethiopian long-distance runner
- March 22
  - Shawn Bradley, American basketball player
  - Cory Lidle, American baseball player (d. 2006)
  - Elvis Stojko, Canadian figure skater
  -

- March 23
  - Joe Calzaghe, Welsh boxer
  - Judith Godrèche, French actress
- March 27
  - Ignacio Garrido, Spanish golfer
  - Charlie Haas, American professional wrestler
  - Jimmy Floyd Hasselbaink, Dutch footballer
  - Ben Richards, British actor (The Bill)
- March 28
  - Nick Frost, English actor, comedian and screenwriter
  - Eby J. Jose, Indian journalist and human rights activist
- March 29
  - Hera Björk, Icelandic singer
  - Junichi Suwabe, Japanese voice actor
- March 30 – Karel Poborský, Czech Republic football player

April

Jennifer Garner

Carmen Electra

Željko Joksimović

- April 3 – Jennie Garth, American actress
- April 4
  - Tag Adams, American pornographic film actor
  - Bastian Pastewka, German comedian and actor
  - Lisa Ray, Canadian model and actress
- April 5 – Junko Takeuchi, Japanese voice actress
- April 6 – Jason Hervey, American actor
- April 8
  - Ariel Hernandez, Cuban boxer
  - Sung Kang, Korean actor
- April 9 – Bernard Ackah, Ivorian mixed martial artist and comedian
- April 10 – Vincent Zhao, Chinese actor and martial artist
- April 11
  - Balls Mahoney, American professional wrestler (d. 2016)
  - Jason Varitek, American baseball player
- April 12 – Şebnem Ferah, Turkish singer and songwriter
- April 13 – Mariusz Czerkawski, Polish ice hockey player
- April 14 – Dean Potter, American free climber (d. 2015)
- April 15 – Arturo Gatti, Canadian boxer (d. 2009)
- April 16 – Conchita Martínez, Spanish tennis player

- April 17
  - Tony Boselli, American football player
  - Jennifer Garner, American actress
  - Muttiah Muralitharan, Sri Lankan cricketer
  - Terran Sandwith, Canadian ice hockey player
- April 19 – Rivaldo, Brazilian footballer
- April 20
  - Lê Huỳnh Đức, Vietnamese footballer
  - Carmen Electra, American actress and singer
  - Željko Joksimović, Serbian singer, composer songwriter, multi-instrumentalist and producer
  - Marko Kon, Serbian composer, producer and singer
  - Stephen Marley, Jamaican-American musician
- April 23 – Choky Ice, Hungarian porn actor
- April 24
  - Chad I Ginsburg, American musician and record producer (CKY)
  - Chipper Jones, American baseball player
- April 26 – Avi Nimni, Israeli footballer
- April 29 – Fredrik Kempe, Swedish songwriter and opera and pop singer
- April 30 – Takako Tokiwa, Japanese actress

May

Dwayne Johnson

The Notorious B.I.G

Ray Whitney

- May 1 – Julie Benz, American actress
- May 2
    - Paul Adcock, English footballer
    - Dwayne Johnson, American professional wrestler and actor
- May 3 – Vyacheslav Kozlov, Russian hockey player
- May 4 – Mike Dirnt, American rock musician and bassist (Green Day)
- May 5 – James Cracknell, British Olympic winning rower
- May 6
    - Janne Blomqvist, Finnish swimmer
    - Martin Brodeur, Canadian hockey goaltender
    - Naoko Takahashi, Japanese long-distance runner
- May 7 – Asghar Farhadi, Iranian film director
- May 8
    - Darren Hayes, Australian musician
    - Ray Whitney, Canadian former NHL player

- May 9
  - Lisa Ann, American pornographic actress
  - Daniela Silivaș, Romanian gymnast
- May 10
  - Radosław Majdan, Polish goalkeeper
  - Katja Seizinger, German alpine skier
- May 15 – Richard Blackwood, English comedian, actor and rapper
- May 16 – Derek Mears, American actor/stuntman
- May 17
  - Tyson Cane, American gay pornographic actor
  - Roman Genn, Russian artist
- May 19
  - Jenny Berggren, Swedish rock singer (Ace of Base)
  - Claudia Karvan, Australian actress
  - Stephanie Nadolny, American voice actress and singer
- May 20
  - Andreas Lundstedt, Swedish singer and actor (Alcazar)
  - Busta Rhymes, African-American rapper and actor
- May 21
  - The Notorious B.I.G., African-American rapper (d. 1997)
  - Kaoru Fujino, Japanese voice actress
- May 22 – Max Brooks, American horror author and screenwriter
- May 23 – Rubens Barrichello, Brazilian race car driver
- May 25
  - Karan Johar, Indian film director, producer, and screenwriter
  - Jules Jordan, American pornographic movie director, actor, and producer

- May 26 – Ahmad Dhani, Indonesian rock musician, songwriter, arranger, and producer
- May 28 – Michael Boogerd, Dutch cyclist
- May 29 – Stanislas Renoult, French singer
- May 30 – Manny Ramírez, Dominican baseball player
- May 31
    - Frode Estil, Norwegian cross-country skier
    - Dave Roberts, American baseball player

June

Wayne Brady

Karl Urban

Ricardo "Rikrok" Ducent

Zinedine Zidane

- June 1 – Rick Gomez, American actor
- June 2 – Wayne Brady, African-American comedian
- June 4
  - Derian Hatcher, American ice hockey player
  - Debra Stephenson, English actress
  - Stoja, Serbian pop-folk singer
- June 5
  - Mike Bucci, American professional wrestler
  - Paweł Kotla, Polish conductor
- June 6 – Cristina Scabbia, Italian singer
- June 7 – Karl Urban, New Zealand actor
- June 8 – Chapman To, Hong Kong actor
- June 10 – Steven Fischer, American film producer and director
- June 14 – Matthias Ettrich, German computer scientist
- June 15 – Andy Pettitte, American baseball player

- June 16 – John Cho, Korean-American actor and musician
- June 17
  - Iztok Čop, Slovenian rower
  - Ricardo "Rikrok" Ducente, British-Jamaican singer
- June 18 – Roger "Infernus" Tiegs, Norwegian black metal musician, original member of Gorgoroth
- June 19 – Jean Dujardin, French actor and comedian
- June 20 – Shane Hamman, American Olympic weightlifter and powerlifter
- June 21 – Irene van Dyk, South African–born netball player
- June 22 – Miguel del Toro, Mexican baseball player
- June 23 – Zinedine Zidane, French footballer
- June 24
  - Robbie McEwen, Australian professional road bicycle racer
  - Denis Žvegelj, Slovenian rower
- June 25 – Carlos Delgado, Puerto Rican baseball player
- June 28 – Jon Heidenreich, American professional wrestler
- June 29
  - Samantha Smith, American peace activist (d. 1985)
  - Nawal Al Zoghbi, Lebanese singer

July

Sofía Vergara

Maya Rudolph

Elizabeth Berkley

Wil Wheaton

- July 3 – Asha Gill, British-born television host
- July 4
  - Alexei Shirov, Spanish chess Grandmaster
  - Craig Spearman, New Zealand cricketer
- July 6 – Mark Gasser, British concert pianist
- July 7
  - Stoney Case, American football player
  - Lisa Leslie, American basketball player
- July 8 – Sourav Ganguly, Indian cricketer
-

- July 10
    - Sofía Vergara, Colombian actress and former TV personality/model
    - Tilo Wolff, German musician
- July 12
    - Travis Best, American basketball player
    - Jake Wood, English actor
- July 13 – Sean Waltman, American professional wrestler
- July 14 – Masami Suzuki, Japanese voice actress
- July 19 – Daedalus Howell, American writer and filmmaker
- July 21 – Catherine Ndereba, Kenyan long-distance runner
- July 22
    - Andrew Holness, 9th Prime Minister of Jamaica
    - Keyshawn Johnson, African-American football player
- July 23 – Marlon Wayans, African-American actor, comedian and producer
- July 26 – Nathan Buckley, Australian rules footballer
- July 27
    - Takako Fuji, Japanese actress
    - Maya Rudolph, African-American actress, comedian
    - Takashi Shimizu, Japanese director
- July 28
    - Elizabeth Berkley, American actress
    - Yum Jung-ah, South Korean actress
- July 29 – Wil Wheaton, American actor
- July 31 – Tami Stronach, Iranian-born dancer and former actress

August

Ben Affleck

Cameron Diaz

- August 1
    - Marc Costanzo, Canadian musician
    - Devon Hughes, American professional wrestler
- August 2
    - Chris Bender, American musician (d. 1991)
    - Kelly Richardson, Canadian contemporary artist
- August 3 – Patrik Isaksson, Swedish singer and songwriter
- August 6 – Geri Halliwell, British pop singer (Spice Girls)
- August 7
    - Sarah Cawood, British television presenter
    - Karen Disher, American voice actress
    - Brad Patton, Swedish pornographic actor
- August 9 – A-mei, Taiwanese singer

- August 10 – Angie Harmon, American actress
- August 11 – Jonathon Prandi, American model and actor
- August 12 – Demir Demirkan, Turkish rock musician and songwriter
- August 13 – Kevin Plank, American entrepreneur (Under Armour)
- August 14
  - Takako Honda, Japanese voice actress
  - Yoo Jae-suk, South Korean comedian and television comedy show host
  - Ed O'Bannon, American basketball player
- August 15
  - Ben Affleck, American actor
  - Mikey Graham, Irish singer (Boyzone)
- August 16
  - Frankie Boyle, Scottish comedian
  - Emily Robison, American country music performer (Dixie Chicks)
- August 17 – Ken Ryker, American pornographic actor
- August 18 – Leo Ku, Hong Kong actor and singer
- August 19 – Sammi Cheng, Hong Kong singer and actress
- August 20 – Chaney Kley, American actor (d. 2007)
- August 22 – Jonathan Coachman, American World Wrestling Entertainment announcer
- August 23 – Anthony Calvillo, Canadian Football League quarterback
- August 25 – Marvin Harrison, American football player
- August 26 – Samar Kokash, Syrian actress and voice actress
- August 27
  - Jimmy Pop, American musician
  - Mike Smith, Canadian actor

- August 29 – Bae Yong-joon, South Korean actor
- August 30
  - Cameron Diaz, American actress
  - Pavel Nedvěd, Czech footballer

September

Gwyneth Paltrow

Dita Von Teese

- September 2 – Sergejs Žoltoks, Latvian hockey player (d. 2004)
- September 4 – Françoise Yip, Chinese-Canadian actress
- September 6 – Anika Noni Rose, American actress
- September 7 – Sean Daley, American hip-hop musician (Atmosphere)
- September 8
  - Lisa Kennedy Montgomery, American disc jockey and political satirist
  - Os du Randt, South African rugby player

- o Tomokazu Seki, Japanese voice actor
- September 9 – Natasha Kaplinsky, English newsreader
- September 10
  - o Sara Groves, American Christian musician
  - o Bledar Sejko, Albanian guitarist, composer, and singer
  - o Ghada Shouaa, Syrian athlete
  - o Rio Tahara, Japanese snowboarder
- September 12 – Budi Putra, Indonesian journalist, writer and blogger
- September 13 – Kelly Chen, Hong Kong actress and singer
- September 15
  - o Queen Letizia of Spain
  - o Jimmy Carr, British comedian
- September 16
  - o Sprent Dabwido, Nauruan politician
  - o Alessandro "Lord Vampyr" Nunziati, Italian singer, record producer and writer (Theatres des Vampires, Cain, Lord Vampyr's Shadowsreign)
- September 17 – Bobby Lee, Asian-American comedian
- September 19
  - o Jim Druckenmiller, National Football League quarterback
  - o Ashot Nadanian, Armenian chess player, theoretician and coach
- September 21
  - o Liam Gallagher, British singer (Oasis)
  - o Jon Kitna, American football player
- September 22 – Matthew Rush, American gay pornographic actor
- September 23
  - o Ana Marie Cox, American author and blogger

- Karl Pilkington, English radio producer
- September 24 – Karyn Bosnak, American author
- September 26 – Shawn Stockman, American singer and musician (Boyz II Men)
- September 27
  - Sylvia Crawley, American basketball player
  - Gwyneth Paltrow, American actress
- September 28 – Dita Von Teese, American burlesque artist
- September 29 – Robert Webb, comedian and actor
- September 30
  - Ari Behn, Norwegian author
  - José Lima, Dominican baseball player (d. 2010)
  - Shaan, Indian singer

October

Eminem

Gabrielle Union

Sandra Kim

Tarkan

- October 1 – Jean Paulo Fernandes, Brazilian footballer
- October 2 – Konstantinos Papadakis, Greek pianist
- October 3
  - Kim Joo-hyuk, South Korean actor
  - Guy Oseary, Israeli-American businessman
- October 4 – Van Darkholme, Vietnamese-American gay pornographic actor, director, and photographer
- October 5
  - Aaron Guiel, Canadian baseball player
  - Grant Hill, African-American basketball player
- October 6
  - Anders Iwers, Swedish musician
  - Ko So-young, South Korean actress
  - J. J. Stokes, American football player
- October 8 – Kim Myung-min, South Korean actor

- October 9 – Etan Patz, missing American schoolboy
- October 10 – Jun Lana, Filipino playwright and screenwriter
- October 11 – Claudia Black, Australian actress
- October 12 – Mechele Linehan, American murderer
- October 15 – Sandra Kim, Belgian singer, Eurovision Song Contest 1986 winner
- October 17
  - Eminem, American rapper and actor
  - Sharon Leal, American actress and director
  - Tarkan, Turkish singer
- October 19 – Sayaka Aoki, Japanese voice actress
- October 21
  - Masakazu Morita, Japanese voice actor
  - Evhen Tsybulenko, Ukrainian professor of international law
- October 22
  - D'Lo Brown, American professional wrestler
  - Saffron Burrows, British actress
- October 24
  - Kim Ji-soo, South Korean actress
  - Scott Peterson, American convicted murderer
  - Pat Williams, American football player
- October 27
  - Lee Clark, English footballer
  - Elissa, Lebanese singer
  - Marika Krook, Finnish singer (Edea)
  - Maria de Lurdes Mutola, Mozambican athlete
  - Brad Radke, American baseball player
- October 28
  - Terrell Davis, American football player

- o Brad Paisley, American country music singer-songwriter
- October 29
  - o Takafumi Horie, Japanese entrepreneur
  - o Tracee Ellis Ross, American actress
  - o Gabrielle Union, American actress
- October 31 – Matt Dawson, English rugby player and TV personality

November

Thandie Newton

Rebecca Romijn

Josh Duhamel

Arjun Rampal

- November 1
  - Mario Barth, German comedian
  - Toni Collette, Australian actress
  - Jenny McCarthy, American actress and model
  - Naoki Yanagi, Japanese voice actor
- November 2
  - Vladimir Vorobiev, Russian ice hockey player
  - Samantha Womack, British actress
- November 4 – Luís Figo, Portuguese footballer
- November 5 – Krassimir Avramov, Bulgarian singer and songwriter
- November 6
  - Thandie Newton, British actress
  - Rebecca Romijn, American actress and model
  - Adonis Georgiades, Greek historian and politician, Greek Minister of Health
- November 7 – Danny Grewcock, British rugby player
- November 8
  - Maja Marijana, Serbian pop-folk singer
  - Gretchen Mol, American actress
- November 9
  - Eric Dane, American actor

- Doug Russell, American sports media personality
- Naomi Shindō, Japanese voice actor
- November 10
  - Lou Brutus, American radio host, musician and photographer
  - Shawn Green, American baseball player
- November 11 – Adam Beach, Canadian actor
- November 13 – Takuya Kimura, Japanese actor
- November 14
  - Matt Bloom, American wrestler
  - Josh Duhamel, American actor and model
  - Jonathan Slinger, British actor
- November 16 – Missi Pyle, American actress and singer
- November 23 – Alf-Inge Håland, Norwegian footballer
- November 26 – Arjun Rampal, Indian actor
- November 28 – Jesper Strömblad, Swedish musician
- November 29 – Andreas Goldberger, Austrian ski jumper
- November 30 – Christopher Fitzgerald, American actor

December

Alyssa Milano

Daniel Alfredsson

Jude Law

- December 4
  - Marc Bator, German journalist and television presenter
  - Yūko Miyamura, Japanese voice actress, actress and singer
- December 5 – Cole Youngblood, American pornographic actor
- December 6 – Mónica Santa María, Peruvian model and TV host (d. 1994)
- December 7
  - Hermann Maier, Austrian skier
  - Tammy Lynn Sytch, American wrestling manager and personality
  - Jason Winer, American actor, comedian, writer, director and producer

- December 9 – Tré Cool, American rock musician and drummer (Green Day)
- December 10 – Brian Molko, American musician (Placebo)
- December 11 – Daniel Alfredsson, Swedish former hockey player
- December 12
  - Wilson Kipketer, Danish athlete
  - Brandon Teena, American murder victim (d. 1993)
- December 13 – Chris Grant, Australian footballer
- December 14 – Miranda Hart, British Comedian and Actress
- December 15
  - Rodney Harrison, American football player
  - Stuart Townsend, Irish actor
- December 16 – Angela Bloomfield, New Zealand actress
- December 17
  - John Abraham, Indian actor
  - Laurie Holden, American-Canadian actress and human rights activist
- December 19
  - Alyssa Milano, American actress
  - Warren Sapp, American football player
- December 22 – Vanessa Paradis, French singer and actress
- December 23
  - Morgan, Italian singer, composer, multi-instrumentalist and X Factor (Italy) judge
  - Christian Potenza, Canadian actor/voice actor
- December 24 – Klaus Schnellenkamp, German-Chilean author
- December 25
  - Josh Freese, American musician and drummer
  - Qu Yunxia, Chinese middle-distance runner

- December 26 – Shane Meadows, English director
- December 27 – Colin Charvis, Welsh rugby player
- December 28
  - Patrick Rafter, Australian tennis player
  - Adam Vinatieri, American football player
- December 29 – Jude Law, British actor
- December 30 – Kerry Collins, American football player
- December 31 – Joey McIntyre, American actor and singer (New Kids on the Block)

Date unknown

- Imaani, English singer, Eurovision Song Contest 1998 runner-up
- Marente de Moor, Dutch writer
- Jakob Martin Strid, Danish cartoonist
- Artur Żurawski, Polish cinematographer and director

Deaths

January

Frederick IX of Denmark

Mahalia Jackson

- January 1 – Maurice Chevalier, French entertainer (b. 1888)
- January 6 – Chen Yi, Chinese communist military commander and politician (b. 1901)
- January 7 – Emma P. Carr, American spectroscopist (b. 1880)
- January 8
    - Edwin Hugh Lundie, American architect (b. 1886)
    - Kenneth Patchen, American poet and painter (b. 1911)
    - Wesley Ruggles, American film director (b. 1889)
- January 9 – Ted Shawn, American dancer (b. 1891)
- January 10 – Aksel Larsen, Danish politician (b. 1897)
- January 14 – King Frederick IX of Denmark (b. 1899)
- January 16 – Ross Bagdasarian, Sr., American record producer (*Alvin and the Chipmunks*) (b. 1919)
- January 17
    - Rochelle Hudson, American actress (b. 1916)
    - Betty Smith, American writer (b. 1896)
- January 18 – Clarence Earl Gideon, Defendant during civil rights court case (*Gideon v. Wainwright*) (b. 1910)
- January 24 – Jerome Cowan, American actor (b. 1897)
- January 25 – Erhard Milch, German field marshal and *Luftwaffe* officer (b. 1892)

- January 26 – Mahalia Jackson, African-American gospel singer (b. 1911)
- January 31 – King Mahendra of Nepal (b. 1920)

February

Maria Goeppert-Mayer

- February 2 – Jessie Royce Landis, American actress (b. 1896)
- February 3 – John Litel, American actor (b. 1892)
- February 4 – Orlando Ward, American general (b. 1891)
- February 5 – Marianne Moore, American poet (b. 1887)
- February 7 – Walter Lang, American film director (b. 1896)
- February 11 – Jan Wils, Dutch architect (b. 1891)
- February 19 – John Grierson, Scottish documentary filmmaker (b. 1898)
- February 20
  - Maria Goeppert-Mayer, German physicist, Nobel Prize laureate (b. 1906)
  - Walter Winchell, American journalist (b. 1897)
- February 21 – Zhang Guohua, Chinese general and politician (b. 1914)
- February 22
  - Tedd Pierce, American animator (b. 1906)
  - Dan Katchongva, Native American traditional leader (b. 1860)
- February 27 – Pat Brady, American actor (b. 1914)

March

- March 4 – Harold Barrowclough, New Zealand general, lawyer, and chief justice (b. 1894)
- March 11
  - Fredric Brown, American science fiction and mystery writer (b. 1906).
  - Zack Wheat, American baseball player (Brooklyn Dodgers) and a member of the MLB Hall of Fame (b. 1888)
- March 13
  - Len Ford, American football player (Cleveland Browns) and a member of the Pro Football Hall of Fame (b. 1926)
  - Tony Ray-Jones, British photographer (b. 1941)
- March 16 – Pie Traynor, American baseball player (Pittsburgh Pirates) and a member of the MLB Hall of Fame (b. 1898)
- March 20 – Marilyn Maxwell, American actress (b. 1921)
- March 21 – David McCallum, Sr., British violinist and father of actor David McCallum (b. 1897)
- March 23 – Cristóbal Balenciaga, Spanish couturier (b. 1895)
- March 27
  - Sharkey Bonano, American jazz musician (b. 1904)
  - M. C. Escher, Dutch artist (b. 1898)
- March 29 – J. Arthur Rank, British industrialist and film producer (b. 1888)

April

Ferde Grofé

Heinrich Lübke

Kwame Nkrumah

- April 2
  - Franz Halder, German general (b. 1884)
  - Gil Hodges, American baseball player (b. 1924)

- April 3 – Ferde Grofé, American pianist and composer (b. 1892)
- April 4
  - Adam Clayton Powell, Jr., African-American politician (b. 1908)
  - Stefan Wolpe, German-born composer (b. 1902)
- April 5
  - Brian Donlevy, American actor (b. 1901)
  - Isabel Jewell, American actress (b. 1907)
- April 6 – Heinrich Lübke, German former president (b. 1894)
- April 7
  - Betty Blythe, American actress (b. 1893)
  - Abeid Karume, President of Zanzibar (b. 1905)
  - August Zaleski, former President of Poland (b. 1883)
- April 9 – James F. Byrnes, United States Secretary of State and Justice of the Supreme Court (b. 1879)
- April 11 – George H. Plympton, American screenwriter (b. 1889)
- April 13 – Dorothy Dalton, American actress (b. 1893)
- April 16 – Yasunari Kawabata, Japanese writer, Nobel Prize laureate (b. 1899)
- April 25 – George Sanders, British actor (b. 1906)
- April 26 – Fernando Amorsolo, Filipino painter (b. 1892)
- April 27 – Kwame Nkrumah, Ghanaian politician (b. 1909)
- April 30 – Gia Scala, English actress (b. 1934)

May

J. Edgar Hoover

King Edward VIII

- May 2 – J. Edgar Hoover, American Federal Bureau of Investigation director (b. 1895)
- May 3 – Bruce Cabot, American actor (b. 1904)
- May 4 – Edward Calvin Kendall, American chemist, recipient of the Nobel Prize in Physiology or Medicine (b. 1886)
- May 5
  - Martiros Saryan, Armenian painter (b. 1880)
  - Frank Tashlin, American film director (b. 1913)
- May 6 – Deniz Gezmiş, Turkish revolutionary (b. 1947)
- May 12 – Steve Ihnat, American actor (b. 1934)
- May 13 – Dan Blocker, American actor (*Bonanza*) (b. 1928)
- May 18 – Sidney Franklin, American film director (b. 1893)
- May 22
  - Cecil Day-Lewis, British poet (b. 1904)
  - Dame Margaret Rutherford, English actress (b. 1892)
- May 23 – Richard Day, Canadian art director (b. 1896)
- May 24
  - Asta Nielsen, Danish silent film actress (b. 1881)
  - Ismail Yassine, Egyptian comedian and actor (b. 1912)

- May 28 – The Duke of Windsor (the former King Edward VIII; b. 1894)
- May 29 – Prithviraj Kapoor, Indian actor and director (b. 1901)
- May 31 – Walter Freeman, American physician (b. 1895)

June

- June 10 – Edward Milford, Australian general (b. 1894)
- June 12
  - Saul Alinsky, American political activist (b. 1909)
  - Ludwig von Bertalanffy, Austrian biologist (b. 1901)
  - Edmund Wilson, American writer and critic (b. 1895)
- June 13
  - Georg von Békésy, Hungarian biophysicist, recipient of the Nobel Prize in Physiology or Medicine (b. 1899)
  - Stephanie von Hohenlohe, Austrian-born German World War II spy (b. 1891)
  - Clyde McPhatter, American singer (b. 1932)
  - Felix Stump, American admiral (b. 1894)
- June 18 – Milton Humason, American astronomer (b. 1891)
- June 22 – Vladimir Durković, Serbian footballer (b. 1937)
- June 25 – Jan Matulka, American painter (b. 1890)

July

- July 2 – Joseph Fielding Smith, 10th president of The Church of Jesus Christ of Latter-day Saints (b. 1876)
- July 6 – Brandon deWilde, American actor (b. 1942)
- July 7 – King Talal of Jordan (b. 1909)
- July 21
  - Ralph Craig, American athlete (b. 1889)

- King Jigme Dorji Wangchuck of Bhutan (b. 1929)
- July 22 – Max Aub, Mexican-Spanish novelist (b. 1903)
- July 24 – Lance Reventlow, American playboy and race car driver (b. 1936)
- July 25 – Américo Castro, Spanish historian and philologist (b. 1885)
- July 27 – Count Richard Nikolaus von Coudenhove-Kalergi, Austrian-Japanese politician, geopolitician and philosopher(b. 1894)
- July 28 – Helen Traubel, American soprano (b. 1903)
- July 31
  - Alfons Gorbach, Austrian politician, former Federal Chancellor (b. 1903)
  - Paul-Henri Spaak, Belgian statesman and diplomat, former Prime Minister and Secretary General of NATO (b. 1899)

August

- August 7
  - Joi Lansing, American actress (b. 1928)
  - Tom Neal, American actor (b. 1914)
- August 8 – Andrea Feldman, American actress (b. 1948)
- August 11 – Max Theiler, South African virologist, recipient of the Nobel Prize in Physiology or Medicine (b. 1899)
- August 14 – Oscar Levant, American pianist and actor (b. 1906)
- August 16 – Pierre Brasseur, French actor (b. 1905)
- August 19
  - Rudolf Belling, German sculptor (b. 1886)
  - James Patterson, American actor (b. 1932)

- August 20 – Harold Rainsford Stark, American admiral (b. 1880)
- August 21 – Heinz Ziegler, German general (b. 1894)
- August 24 – Jinichi Kusaka, Japanese admiral (b. 1888)
- August 25 – Juan Carlos Paz, Argentine composer and music theorist (b. 1901)
- August 26 – Francis Chichester, British sailor and aviator (b. 1901)
- August 27 – Yung Fung-shee, Hong Kong philanthropist (b. 1900)
- August 28 – Prince William of Gloucester (b. 1941)
- August 29 – René Leibowitz, French composer (b. 1913)

September

- September 1 – He Xiangning, Chinese revolutionary, feminist, politician, painter and poet (b. 1878)
- September 2 – Ivan Yumashev, Soviet admiral (b. 1895)
- September 5 (Munich massacre):
  - Yossef Romano, Israeli weightlifter (b. 1940)
  - Moshe Weinberg, Israeli wrestling coach (b. 1939)
- September 6 (Munich massacre):
  - David Mark Berger, Israeli weightlifter (b. 1944)
  - Ze'ev Friedman, Israeli weightlifter (b. 1944)
  - Yossef Gutfreund, Israeli wrestling referee (b. 1932)
  - Eliezer Halfin, Israeli wrestler (b. 1948)
  - Amitzur Shapira, Israeli athletics coach (b. 1932)
  - Kehat Shorr, Israeli shooting coach (b. 1919)
  - Mark Slavin, Israeli wrestler (b. 1954)
  - Andre Spitzer, Israeli fencing coach (b. 1945)
  - Yakov Springer, Israeli weightlifting judge (b. c. 1921)

- September 8 – Warren Kealoha, American Olympic swimmer (b. 1904)
- September 11 – Max Fleischer, American animator (b. 1883)
- September 12 – William Boyd, American actor (b. 1895)
- September 14 – Lane Chandler, American actor (b. 1899)
- September 15
  - Geoffrey Fisher, Archbishop of Canterbury (b. 1887)
  - H. Kent Hewitt, American admiral (b. 1887)
- September 17
  - Thomas L. Sprague, American admiral (b. 1894)
  - Akim Tamiroff, Russian actor (b. 1899)
- September 19 – Robert Casadesus, French pianist (b. 1899)
- September 21 – Henry de Montherlant, French writer (b. 1896)
- September 26
  - Charles Correll, American radio actor (b. 1890)
  - Robert E. Dolan, American composer (b. 1906)

October

Louis Leakey

Igor Sikorsky

- October 1 – Louis Leakey, British paleontologist (b. 1903)
- October 5 – Ivan Yefremov, Soviet paleontologist and science fiction author (b. 1907)
- October 9
  - Dave Bancroft, American baseball player (Cleveland Indians) and a member of the MLB Hall of Fame (b. 1891)
  - Miriam Hopkins, American actress (b. 1902)
- October 16 – Leo G. Carroll, English actor (b. 1886)
- October 18 – Esma Cannon, British actress (b. 1905)
- October 20 – Harlow Shapley, American astronomer (b. 1885)
- October 24
  - Jackie Robinson, African-American baseball player (Brooklyn Dodgers) and a member of the MLB Hall of Fame (b. 1919)
  - Claire Windsor, American actress (b. 1892)
- October 26 – Igor Sikorsky, Russian aviation engineer (b. 1889)
- October 28 – Mitchell Leisen, American film director (b. 1898)
- October 29 – Victor Milner, American cinematographer (b. 1893)

November

Ezra Pound

- November 1 – Ezra Pound, American poet (b. 1885)
- November 3 – Harry Richman, American entertainer (b. 1895)
- November 5 – Reginald Owen, English actor (b. 1887)
- November 12 – Rudolf Friml, Czech composer (b. 1879)
- November 13 – Margaret Webster, American actress (b. 1905)
- November 14 – Martin Dies, Jr., American politician (b. 1900)
- November 17 – Thomas C. Kinkaid, American admiral (b. 1888)
- November 18 – Danny Whitten, American musician (b. 1943)
- November 23 – Marie Wilson, American actress (b. 1916)
- November 25 – Henri Coandă, Romanian aerodynamics pioneer (b. 1886)
- November 28 – Havergal Brian, English composer (b. 1876)
- November 29 – Carl Stalling, American composer (b. 1891)
- November 30 – Hans Erich Apostel, Austrian composer (b. 1901)

December

Harry Truman

Lester B. Pearson

- December 1
    - Antonio Segni, Italian politician who was the 34th Prime Minister of Italy (1955–1957, 1959–1960), and the fourth President of the Italian Republic (b. 1891)
    - Andreas Tzimas, Greek communist politician and Resistance leader (b. 1909)
- December 2
    - Ettore Bastico, Italian field marshal (b. 1876)
    - José Limón, Mexican choreographer (b. 1908)
    - Yip Man, master of Wing Chun Kung Fu (b. 1893)
- December 3 – Bill Johnson, American musician (b. 1872)
- December 6 – Janet Munro, British actress (b. 1934)
-

- December 9
    - William Dieterle, German film director (b. 1893)
    - Louella Parsons, American gossip columnist (b. 1881)
- December 12 – Thomas H. Robbins, Jr., American admiral (b. 1900)
- December 15 – Edward Earle, Canadian actor (b. 1882)
- December 20 – Gabby Hartnett, American baseball player (Chicago Cubs) and a member of the MLB Hall of Fame (b. 1900)
- December 21 – Paul Hausser, German Waffen SS general (b. 1880)
- December 22 – Jimmy Wallington, American radio personality (b. 1907)
- December 23 — Andrei Tupolev, Soviet aircraft designer (b. 1888).
- December 24
    - Charles Atlas, Italian-American strongman and sideshow performer (b. 1892)
    - Gisela Richter, English art historian (b. 1882)
    - Daniel McVey, Australian public servant (b. 1892)
- December 25 – C. Rajagopalachari, Indian politician and freedom-fighter. Last Governor-General of India (1948–50) (b. 1878)
- December 26 – Harry S. Truman, 33rd President of the United States (b. 1884)
- December 27 – Lester B. Pearson, 14th Prime Minister of Canada, recipient of the Nobel Peace Prize (b. 1897)
- December 28 – Link Lyman, American football player (Chicago Bears) and a member of the Pro Football Hall of Fame (b. 1898)

- December 31 – Roberto Clemente, Puerto Rican baseball player (Pittsburgh Pirates) and a member of the MLB Hall of Fame (b. 1934)

Nobel Prizes

- Physics – John Bardeen, Leon Neil Cooper, John Robert Schrieffer
- Chemistry – Christian B. Anfinsen, Stanford Moore, William H. Stein
- Physiology or Medicine – Gerald M. Edelman, Rodney R. Porter
- Literature – Heinrich Böll
- Peace – not awarded
- Economics – John Hicks, Kenneth Arrow

In the News

General Idi Amin of Uganda expells 50,000 Asians From Uganda.

Richard Nixon Visits China.

American Swimmer Mark Spitz wins a record 7 gold medals in the Summer Olympics in Munich.

The Winter Olympic Games are held in Sapporo, Japan.

Popular Films - The Godfather. Fiddler on the Roof. Diamonds Are Forever, What's Up, Doc?, Dirty Harry.

11 Israel Athletes murdered by Arab Gunman at Munich Olympics.

Five White House operatives are arrested for burglarizing the offices of the Democratic National Committee the start of the Watergate Scandal.

16 survivors from plane crash survive and are rescued after practicing cannibalism.

Bobby Fischer beats Boris Spassky to become the World Chess Champion in Reykjavik, Iceland.

Last US ground troops withdrawn from Vietnam.

The last major epidemic of smallpox in Europe breaks out in Yugoslavia.

The worlds leaders agree to banning biological warfare.

The ex RMS Queen Elizabeth Sets on Fire and Sinks in Hong Kong.

General Idi Amin of Uganda expells 50,000 Asians From Uganda.

The Largest Diamond The Star of Sierra leone is unearthed it is 969.8 carats.